So You Want to be a Teacher

So You Want to be a Teacher

Ian Marcus Dyer

ATHENA PRESS
LONDON

ISBN 978 1 84748 656 1

First published 2009 by
ATHENA PRESS
Queen's House, 2 Holly Road
Twickenham TW1 4EG
United Kingdom

Printed for Athena Press

To Dot and Keith
For their help, advice and friendship

Foreword

Ian Dyer first impinged upon my life in 1961 when at morning assembly the list of boys condemned to detention would be read out. 'Anslow – two hours, Dyer – two hours, Glendenning – two hours.' Who was this weedy specimen, and how did he manage so consistently to transgress the standards and traditions of a proud 400-year-old school? The problem was that, let us just say, Ian Dyer was not Oxbridge material. Nevertheless, those charged with his education presumed that this matter was capable of rectification by the mere process of forcing him to spend two hours on a Wednesday afternoon writing out 500 times 'I must not…' (whatever the sin was). How little they knew.

However, while trigonometry, chemical equations and the acts and antics of William Pitt proved to be of little interest to Ian, he would never have been happier than if the single weekly forty-five-minute period of biology had commenced at nine o'clock on a Monday and ended last thing on a Friday afternoon. In a tribute to Charles Darwin, Ian adapted rapidly to his environment, grew big and strong and began to observe the world. Over the next four or five years he borrowed my bike and my airgun, while I borrowed his fishing rod, smoked his Woodbines and blew him up with an experimental cannon. Just normal stuff, really, in those halcyon days when we knew less about Health and Safety than we knew about *Health and Efficiency*.

In time, his tormentors perhaps gave him up as a lost educational cause and allowed him every other Wednesday off. I like to think that one or two of those gentlemen, hardbitten from what they had been required to do in the 1940s in defence of the realm, reluctantly recognised that in Ian's irrepressibility there lurked the spirit that could keep colleagues' hopes alive as he flouted authority in some POW camp – or worse – a school staffroom. And that was the astonishing thing. With all those careers open to him – diamond smuggling, explosives demolition or strapping radio collars to crocodiles on Lake Tanganyika, he chose teaching.

But he didn't choose teaching in the leafy suburbs, building Utopia for the heirs of the captains of industry. He chose to spend his working life where educational aspiration was at its lowest. He chose to open a window on life for children who would receive little encouragement from home. Perhaps he only changed the lives of one in a hundred and suffered for the ninety-nine, but I am sure that he will be remembered by honest staff and those adults who were once children under his care as a bloody good teacher, with his heart and his motivation in exactly the right place.

As you read Ian's verdict on education, spare a thought for a devalued profession and ask yourself who benefits by not letting good teachers teach, by shackling them with the endless chains of regulations, procedures, experimental theories and limitless reports, plans, forms and statistical bullshit. We aren't so smart any more. Even a herdsman on the shores of Lake Tanganyika knows that if you want your goats to get fat, you need to feed them, not keep weighing them all the time.

Perhaps it's time for a change. But if not now, when? If not you, who?

Peter Handley

Contents

The Prologue

If teachings the job that you choose,
Go on, you have nothing to lose
Please don't be put off
While reading this guff,
Put your tongue in your cheek and peruse.

Have you achieved good standards academically? Do you have a wide range of interests? Do you have a passion for music and the arts? Are you a keen sportsperson? Do you enjoy sharing your talents and enthusiasm with others? Do you have a sense of achievement when your love of nature is appreciated and taken on by others? Is teaching for you?

Be very careful!

I started teaching in 1971 as part of the vast army of teachers trained in the sixties and early seventies. The first twenty years of my career were in some ways idyllic. Although I was expected to ensure the progress of my children in what are now known as the core subjects, I still had opportunities to share my passions with the pupils under my care. The children, believe it or not, showed progress in all areas and both standards and expectations were high. Many of the children I taught became teachers, nurses, actors and at least one a current member of parliament. I taught at an 'ordinary' primary school with 'ordinary children'. The one thing that stays in my mind is that I enjoyed every day at school; I looked forward to getting back after school holidays and had a tremendous sense of achieving something worthwhile.

So what has gone wrong? Why are teachers of my generation leaving the profession in droves? I think that a great deal of what was once part of a highly rewarding job has now been either taken out of our hands completely or has been so devalued that it has faded into obscurity, all in the name of 'improving standards'. A lot of this was caused by that recipe for mediocrity, 'The National

Curriculum', a concept so wonderful that it went through more regenerations than Doctor Who. How many of us remember the countless staff meetings dedicated to devising the dreaded tick charts? The googols of attainment targets that keen types could recite verbatim. But worse was yet to come. Lurking on the horizon were SATs, League tables, target setting and a host of other incomprehensible (and useless) innovations. Of course, none of this could have happened if it had not been for the evolution of several new species including: the Advanced Skills Teacher (AST), the Advisory Teacher (AT) and by far and away the most terrifying, the Power Dressing Head (PDH) – motto: *Excrementum Tauri Imperat OK.*

The latter are usually, but not of necessity, female, have little sense of humour, the people management skills of Attila the Hun and have great difficulty in choosing the correct face to use. Their one saving grace is that they are either out of school, spreading the message or locked in their inner sanctum planning further 'improvements'.

ATs and ASTs come from a variety of backgrounds. In some cases they are actually very good, offer sound advice and can actually do the job. Unfortunately these are rare. The rest fall into two main groups, namely the 'I was made redundant when my school was closed,' and, 'I can do one lesson very well and if I play my cards right I can do it in several thousand schools before I'm found out.' The ASTs usually gain their posts by spending inordinate amounts of time in the inner sanctum with the PDH. As a supply teacher I observed the same AST leading staff meetings on AL (accelerated learning) in a number of schools using exactly the same script. I still have to find a use for being able to count to ten in Japanese, as this is about all I can remember from these inspirational courses.

Now, getting back to the rise of the PDH. In my first five years of teaching I cannot remember having one formal staff meeting. Strange, isn't it, that everybody knew exactly what was going on in the school? I now believe that the rarity of meetings was because the then head teachers had not correctly grasped the latest methods of curing insomnia in the staffroom. (Grasped, or perhaps I should say GRASP (Getting Results And Solving

Problems). The answer came, of course, with the rise of the abbreviation and the acronym. It did not take many minutes for a skilled PDH to induce deep coma in an entire staff by using a language entirely alien to the PUT (Poor Unsuspecting Teacher). Remember KS1, KS2, QCA, SATs, SENCO and GRASP, GEST, LMS et al., not to mention GROPE (Getting Results from Other People's Efforts). I'm afraid that we have gone too far down these avenues for the 'Campaign for the Realistic Approach to Pedagogy' to have any effect whatsoever.

'What about the pay and all those holidays?' I hear you ask. As for the holidays, believe me you need them. Just take a look at the parents' faces when they hand their children over to your tender care after the summer break – and they just have one or two in their charge! The matter of salary is a more complex case. Personally, up until a few years ago I had few complaints in this direction. The salary was not great but in true Micawberish fashion I could lead a comfortable lifestyle. Then came perhaps the most divisive scheme introduced by a government, namely 'The Threshold' – UP1, UP2, UP3. At first sight what a wonderful idea; let's reward the PUT by putting him on a higher rate for working hard and achieving results. In many schools it did work, that is, those with an EHT (Enlightened Head Teacher), but often, if you had a PDH in charge, it was a different matter.

I worked at a school where more than half of the staff were not considered good enough. The system relied on your ability to produce evidence. No longer was your word as a qualified, experienced and highly trained professional acceptable. The PDH had, for the first time, direct control over your level of income and therefore quality of life and job satisfaction. In fact, he or she could quite legally call you a liar. A similar thing is now happening to the old scheme of management points whereby your salary was paid according to your curriculum responsibility, a post for which you were formally interviewed, and expected to have a certain level of knowledge and expertise. The financial reward was not particularly great but that of job satisfaction often was. These have been replaced by TLRs (Teaching and Learning Responsibilities). If anyone could explain to me what improvements these have introduced I would be most grateful. All of this has ostensibly been introduced to improve standards.

Standards! Now there's a moot point. Standards in learning? Standards in behaviour? Standards in social skills? Back in the 1970s, social skills were considered an important part of education, especially in primary schools. Take just one example. Teachers undertook a lunchtime duty and this generally resulted in children with good table manners. Nowadays the dining hall often resembles feeding time at the zoo, and the task of clearing up one of the labours of Heracles. Rather than using plates and bowls, children are expected to eat from trays that look as if they were bought from the local do-it-yourself store to sort nuts, bolts and washers. One of the reasons that teacher supervision and proper family meals were stopped was the high cost of giving the teachers a free school meal (approximate cost then of thirty pence). Improvements in standards, or a retrograde step?

Standards of behaviour? You will hear it argued that these have not changed – rubbish. On the whole, thirty years ago, children would not openly use foul and abusive language within earshot of a member of staff. Now it is not uncommon for this to be directed at the teacher. Violence from the poor dears is considered a manifestation of some of their deep-seated problems, yet if a teacher breathes too heavily near them they are immediately under suspicion of GBH. The PUT has to be extremely wary in this area, for once again his/her word will usually be totally disbelieved. The LLTs (Lying Little Toerags) however, will be offered counselling, psychiatric help for the mental trauma they have undergone and an assurance that the offending PUT will be hanged, drawn and quartered.

To say that the behaviour of children, sorry, students in some secondary schools resembles that seen in a zoo is a gross insult to the animal kingdom. I worked as a supply teacher at a comprehensive school in a supposedly upmarket area. The attitude and behaviour of a large number of children was absolutely appalling. Yet what can the PUT do? Unfortunately, unless there is support from senior staff, absolutely nothing. Some heads will not exclude pupils for offences that at one time would have had them sent to the colonies. Most teachers fully support inclusion of children who have physical or learning problems, but the inclusion of 'behaviourally challenged' individuals gradually erodes the ethos of the whole school.

What about academic standards? A succession of governments have come to the conclusion that testing children from their arrival in the delivery suite to their point of exit from academia will inevitably result in a universal improvement in standards. In fact all children will be well above average! The kudos this would bring a government is considered well worth the unnecessary stress it inflicts on children, teachers and parents. Pressures put on schools to climb that ridiculous and useless piece of statistical nonsense, 'The League Table' have resulted in other chunks of joy and fun being removed from education. SATs rule OK appears to be the order of the day. Children are having booster classes, revision lessons, and practice papers pushed down their accommodating little throats until they become heartily sick of school. Perhaps if the powers that be could see an eleven-year-old child in tears through worry about their SATs results they may regain a little of their senses. If, however, a school does not produce the goods, the dreaded Ofsted rears its ugly head.

How is it that standards appear to improve year upon year? Easy: a little manipulation of threshold scores and a tweaking of acceptable answers, especially in an election year, can achieve remarkable improvements; ask any SATs paper marker. And talking about markers… I wonder if the general public realises the cost of these examinations. Markers, Team Leaders etc. get paid extremely well to produce an examination result that a self-respecting PUT could have predicted anyway.

There are still rewards to be had from the job. Currently I am working in a school that has the well-being of the children at its heart. We have an EHT, the deputy is great and standards and expectations are high. As far as is possible, SATs and League Tables etc. are kept in their proper place. The staff have managed to maintain their sense of humour and the children are polite, well mannered and well behaved. But having said this, I have had enough. I started here after a period of time as a supply teacher and after three happy years I am taking early retirement. I shall probably work in a few schools as a supply teacher and watch with interest any future 'improvements' in education.

Beware, you prospective teachers. You won't have the same opportunities I have been lucky enough to experience, and you will probably have to work to the age 103 to qualify for an actuarially reduced pension. You won't have the time to enjoy the fun aspects of the job as you will be too busy producing reams of planning, reports, IEPs (Individual Education Programmes) and other assorted (and unnecessary) paperwork. You won't be able to enjoy the spontaneous aspect of the job. A nature walk is out of the question, as by the time you have filled in risk assessments, insurance checks and applied for permission from parents, aunts and second cousins, any desire to go will have evaporated. I am afraid the PDH appears to be an ever-growing threat, aided and nobly abetted by a government that appears to have no idea of the educational direction it is taking. At the moment it is definitely downhill, and I see little hope of recovery. So think hard; examine other possibilities such as stacking supermarket shelves, and if you finally take the plunge may I wish you the very best of luck.

As for me, I'm just going out of education; I may be some time. Goodbye…

Ian M Dyer
Primary school teacher, musician, potter and beekeeper

Now you've gone and done it

So now you're a teacher, BEd
But don't let it go to your head,
As now it's your mission
To find a position –
So some of your debts can be shed.

OK, so you've ignored my sound advice and taken the plunge. You have undergone four years of training. (Now there's a conundrum; some of the best teachers with whom I have been privileged to work were trained for two years. I was trained for three years, with the option of a fourth year to do a degree course. Now it's four years. One wonders why.) However, you will have reached decision point; you are horrendously in debt (again, something that never used to occur when all governments truly believed in education, education, education), so you need a job, and soon.

Where to teach? Choosing a school is not as straightforward as you may think. Don't fall into the trap of thinking, *What a lovely area – these must be lovely kids*. I am afraid that this does not follow. You are more likely to find that the children believe that the world owes them an education, and teachers are of the same worth as what one scrapes off the bottom of one's shoe. Parents at these schools can give you inordinate amounts of grief. They will undoubtedly think that their little Emma or Julian will be God's gift to Oxbridge, and any hint that their child's IQ is closer to that of a marsupial than a Mensa candidate will result in letters to the LEA, MP et al. In a similar vein, don't think you are going to perform miracles with the year six bottom set in Gallows Road Academy. Sidney Poitier may have performed miracles and John Alderton worked wonders; you will not, and will end up frustrated, angry and disillusioned.

On the whole the school building itself has little effect on its quality. I have enjoyed working in a range of buildings from the Victorian era up to the present day and most styles have points in their favour.

In the 1930s, when fresh air was considered healthy, schools were built with long open verandas and large glass doors that could be flung open wide in the long, hazy days of summer. Unfortunately in the winter this style resulted in hyperthermia in children and staff alike. It would be an interesting study to investigate how many fingers and toes were lost to frostbite. They were also carefully designed and positioned so all the class occupants would be blinded by the sunlight at any time of the day. In more modern times, the verandas have been bricked in and blinds installed, and on the whole they provide a decent workplace. There is also the bonus that owing to the apparent mania of that time for cloakrooms and storerooms, there are lots of little cubbyholes where you can hide. Some schools have staff on their payrolls that haven't been seen for years.

The post-war period produced a rash of steel-framed schools with corridors several miles in length and windows like portholes. They were built to accommodate the children of the baby boom years. Usually they had lovely large classrooms and halls but often felt a little lacking in soul.

In the late sixties or early seventies, the open-plan style became in vogue. Why, beggars belief. There were all sorts of educational arguments produced, often by people who should have known better, but the simple fact of the matter was that they were cheap, built of painted breeze blocks and are now looking decidedly shabby. Schools tried to improve the matter by walling up the 'work bases' and installing doors. The end result were tiny classrooms, often with no windows. In one school in my locality the year two classes are housed in one long barn that looks very much like a loft conversion. I was told that it was so unbearably hot in the summer months they have, at great expense, installed air conditioning. This same 'learning base' was so acoustically perfect that a quiet reading lesson was virtually impossible.

To find your way around these schools requires at least a scale diagram and preferably a global positioning system.

One of the best guides to picking your first school is to

examine the staff (discreetly) on pre-interview visits. Pick the oldest and most miserable looking member of staff and then play him/her as you would a prize salmon. Don't, I repeat *don't* ask stupid questions such as, 'Do you enjoy teaching here?' These will almost certainly draw looks of hostile suspicion of the 'Is this young feller me lad/lass an undercover Ofsted agent sort?' followed by a look of disbelief and pity.

Most teachers of twenty-five-years-plus experience find it inexplicable that anyone would think there is any enjoyment left in the profession. However, they can, if you read between the lines, give you a feel as to how content the staff are and what the management is like – crucial points indeed. For goodness sake avoid the twenty- or thirty-something power dresser, who breezes about the school with folder/clipboard/attaché case clasped to his/her bosom. According to them, this will be the best school in Christendom, the children are all delightful although some have their little problems (usually requiring high levels of medication and two or three muscular minders). This type usually has minimal teaching responsibilities and ambitions of management, i.e. zero teaching responsibilities with as little contact with children as possible.

It is really important to find out exactly what is expected from the staff as regards paperwork, planning and attendance at staff meetings/training days. This does vary from school to school. Again casual cross-examination of staff can help you here. The hours that a teacher is expected to put in are very much open to dispute. There is a little clause somewhere in teachers' conditions of service that a head can ask teachers to do any work that is necessary in time laid down by the school. Again, what some think is actually essential to do the job is considered by others to be of no benefit whatsoever to the children or staff. If you find a school where the head is well liked and respected by children and staff, who expects a sensible level of planning and preparation and is approachable – check his age. Remember, if he is about to disappear into the utopia of retirement he or she may be replaced by a PDH. At a stroke these can ruin what has taken a great length of time to build.

A good approach is to consider schools where you carried out your teaching practices. Which did you enjoy working in most, and why? You will be very lucky to get a job in one you did really like, as the ordinary blackboard standard teacher will need prising from their position with a set of tyre levers. However, it is always a possibility. At least it will give you a good insight into what to look for in prospective places of employment.

Be on your guard against Student Councils! In a well-balanced school these appear just before Ofsted inspections and vanish shortly afterwards. However, certain schools consider them the bee's knees. If on entering a school you spot a display of happy, glowing little faces staring at you from the notice board in the entrance hall, 'ware quislings'! Children are children, and will manipulate their peers and their teacher to their own ends. For example, 'Please, Miss [substitute name of head teacher], Mr Brown makes us work too hard in [substitute subject] and we [in other words the LLT] don't think it's fair.' Invariably the child's word will be treated as Holy Scripture, and the result will be either an interview with the head of the 'don't be too hard on the little angels' type, or an obscure reference to the matter at a staff meeting, which will leave no one in any doubt as to which teacher it's aimed at.

In many of the schools where I have worked the relationship between staff and children is such that there is no need for a Student Council. If the children have a problem there is always a member of staff who will listen, and in a good school the pupil–staff relationships will have been so nurtured that if a member of staff has a problem the children will listen. When visiting prospective schools, look for these relationships; they are of infinitely greater worth than quasi-democratic nonsense.

A very good indication of a happy school can be found outside the curriculum. My own belief is that if a school has a thriving sporting and musical life there isn't much wrong with it. Sport, music – in fact any sort of well-run club activities – help you build relationships that will last a lifetime. I regularly meet ex-pupils who remember very little of their day-to-day classroom experiences but fondly remember the plays, the concerts, the football matches and so on.

Watch out for schools that apparently cover every sport and

hobby under the sun. 'Oh yes, our children have always taken part in the rugby/lacrosse/golf tournaments and practise t'ai chi every morning before starting on their daily programme of study...' (for 'programme of study' refer to Chapter 4 – PPP – 'Policies and planning – a plethora of piffle').

All too often these activities will consist of taster sessions conducted by outside agencies with non-qualified teachers as coaches. This has come about as a result of governmental panic that sport is dying out in schools. Believe me, this is nothing more than lip service. Look for schools with established clubs run by experienced and dedicated school staff, and never hold back from offering your services to form a club where you can teach your own interests or perhaps assist at an established one. You will find it hard to find the time at first, especially taking into account the reams of useless 'bull' you will be expected to produce, but it is worth it. Children are crying out for anything that will alleviate the bland monotony of the National Curriculum, and as I have already stated they will gain life-lasting experiences.

You will no doubt by now have come across countless vacancies and read the job description that goes with them. In the good old days it may have read something like this:

Gallows Road Primary School

Required for September:
Class teacher for a year three class. Interest in flower arranging/football an advantage.

Apply to etc., etc.

A description for the same job will now read:

Gallows Road Primary School, Nursery and Space Technology College

Required as soon as is superhumanly possible:
We are looking for a highly motivated, outstanding teacher to work with our highly successful Year Three Team. You will be enthusiastic, passionate and innovative and be prepared to work all the hours God sends. Etc., etc.

Believe me, these descriptions are based on a real job description I have recently read.

Don't be put off, and remember to follow all the pointers I have tried to give you.

Apply for as many positions as you possibly can and hope to get short-listed for the posts you really fancy. When you do get an interview and you really want the job, work at it – walk the local area (wearing a flak jacket if necessary) to get a feel of the environment and the school. Try and spot the head teacher's little foibles. It will give you a good background start in the interview. Dress smartly but, especially if a member of the fairer sex, do not try and outdo the PDH. You will definitely be considered as a threat. Err more towards Anne Robinson rather than Anne Summers.

During the interview always smile, and laugh at any light quips (real or imagined) thrown by the panel. You will be asked questions that you will have really strong opinions about; keep them to yourself. Innovative ideas such as the reintroduction of capital punishment to primary schools may endear you to the hearts of many of the staff but will not put you in the running for the job. You will also be asked questions that you simply do not understand. Don't worry; there is a very good chance this applies to the rest of the panel as well.

You may well be asked if you have any questions. My one lasting regret is that I once declined this offer. I had been pestered by one interviewer, whom I shall refer to as 'Tsar Ivan'. I was aware that he did not approve of my presence on the shortlist. He kept asking the same unanswerable question. I should have thrown caution to the wind and asked what he would have done in that situation. I know for a fact that he wouldn't have had the faintest idea. I still wouldn't have got the job but would have glowed inwardly for years. Ah well... perhaps in my next incarnation. If your questions are invited and you want the job, either respectfully decline or have a mentally prepared list of innocuous (but intelligent) questions.

Anyway, the very best of luck, and if you are successful, read on.

The first day, the first week, the first year

It seems to appear at first sight
That Herod was probably right –
If experience you lack
Then just watch your back,
And gird up your loins for the fight!

Undoubtedly the most terrifying experience one undergoes in a teaching career is the first time you stand in front of a class. Usually this will be on teaching practice and will be doubly daunting, not because of the children, but the class teacher, whom you believe is hanging onto your every word. I was lucky enough, on my first teaching practice, to have a class teacher who discreetly disappeared through the door and left me to it. I have no doubt at all that she was never many metres away just in case some recalcitrant child needed removing by the lugholes – a little trick one was allowed to perform in those days. The same lady also managed to give me a three-minute warning if the college tutor appeared!

However, you are now in a completely different situation. You are standing in a class and they are yours and yours alone and you have to make your mark. Day one can be a make or break experience. You have to lay down your ground rules, learn the names and habits of as many children as you can, and most importantly, survive until home time.

Before we proceed it is important to understand the management system of the school. You are probably under the misconception that the pinnacle of the hierarchy is the head, with his/her wonderful senior management team. These, you think, are closely followed by the 'phase coordinators' (another new term that has crept in through the back door). Staff with responsibilities for different subject areas come next, and finally, you, an NQT, are firmly placed at the bottom of the pecking order. How wrong you are! The real person in charge is the school secretary! She will show you the ropes; tell you where things are kept and where the best places to hide can be found. Nothing that takes place in the school will be successful unless she is 100 per cent behind it, and don't forget, she is the keeper of that wonderful emblem of power, *the telephone*. Always keep on her best side. Ply her with compliments; find out her favourite chocolate and wine and comment on her youth and good looks. This will always keep you at the head of the queue when you need a little typing doing or a coach trip organised.

In second place, but only just, is the caretaker, or 'site manager' as they now prefer to be called. In many schools they are on a par with the secretary and share the honours of leadership. Last, but by no means least, are the cleaners. If you are as untidy as I am you need to build up a special relationship with them. Don't forget they are paid a pittance for performing minor miracles at the end of the day. Often being locals, they are usually a very good source of information and gossip and can sometimes be persuaded to make you a cup of coffee. Always remember, however, that the backbone of the school – the vertebrae – are the classroom teachers, and whatever the head dictates or the management delegate, the school swims or sinks in their domain.

Now back to the classroom. First, very important this, find a person whom you can call on in times of need. It may be the teacher in the next classroom. Ascertain which child can be trusted to summon aid. Don't choose the 'I'm very helpful and know where everything is in the classroom' type. Go for the one who politely sits down with their lips closed awaiting further instructions. It probably will not come to this but it's best to be prepared.

Second, do not attempt to be friendly, or perhaps I should say don't let them become too friendly with you. As a shark can detect a drop of blood from miles away, the children will scent an easy victim. You will be able to establish friendly relationships eventually but it will take time and needs to be on *your* terms and not the children's.

Much the same applies to relationships with parents. Beware the caring mother who tells you how pleased she is that her little

Craig is in your class, as he never got on with Miss Smith last year. You are likely to find that darling little Craig didn't get on with Mr Brown or Mr Jones in previous years, and that the core problem is that our little Craig probably affords great rectal discomfort. You will be dealing with parents a great deal and you will soon learn to recognise the ones to trust.

You may draw the short straw and be on playground duty on your first day. This is highly unlikely but it could happen. If you aren't, then I would strongly advise that you bite the bullet and go out anyway. Learning the routines will pay dividends in the weeks to come. You will soon get used to the flocks of five-year-olds throwing their arms about you and declaring undying love. Dealing with little problems like 'Please, miss, Mary won't play with me,' or 'Please, sir, John called me a w—r!' require a little more care. Watch the experts deal with these situations and learn. I will never forget a charming lady, a very good teacher but rather naïve was confronted with the latter complaint. 'Please Miss Smythe,' (not the real name) 'George just called me a w—r.' Miss Smythe rose to her full four feet ten and replied, 'Well there's nothing wrong with that, is there? Go away and play nicely!'

When she was enlightened later on that day by a sympathetic colleague – me, actually – her reaction was a glory to behold.

On those days when you are not on playground duty, don't spend your time in the classroom, take a break; you need it a) to have a cup of coffee and fulfil the calls of nature, and b) to vent your spleen on the matters of the morning. The same applies to lunchtime. You may need to do a bit of clearing up and get ready for the afternoon, but do have a good break.

You will probably have been to the first staff meeting of the term and been embarrassingly introduced to the rest of the staff. The first meeting usually isn't too bad, but a few points need to be followed for meetings during the rest of the term. As I pointed out in the Prologue, during my first five years of teaching there was not one single formal staff meeting. At break times all the staff, apart from those on duty, went to the staffroom for a break. Anything that needed to be organised was sorted out over a cup of coffee.

For example, some of the best sports days and swimming galas that I have been privileged to help with were sorted in ten minutes. This doesn't mean to say that the staff treated them lightly; the real organisation, carried on after the initial meeting, was far more practical than it is today and therefore worked. There didn't seem to be any 'issues' (God, how I hate that word) that needed to be discussed for hour upon hour. Any real problems were sorted out by the head in his office with any teachers directly involved.

Your first staff meeting won't be too bad, something of a novelty in fact. The same probably could said be for the first two or three. It will not be long, however, before you realise that staff meetings ramble on about the same thing for week after week after week. Nothing of importance is changed, the same staff will utter the same platitudes and the same staff will gently fall asleep. Occasionally you will have a guest speaker to train you in what happens to be on the bandwagon at the current time. At one of these meetings there were three gentlemen sat next to each other on the armless, sponge cushioned chairs that were prevalent in staff rooms at the time (one of these gents was me). The guest speaker was an advisory teacher with responsibilities for science. Anyway, we'd had a long day, the sun was streaming through the windows and we inevitably dozed off with our heads on each other's shoulders. The only people who appeared to take notice were the staff, the guest speaker being apparently oblivious. We weren't ever allowed to forget the occasion. At a similar meeting when we were being instructed in 'Reading Recovery' (personal tuition at a one-to-one level for children who couldn't be bothered to listen the first time), this time the head himself dropped off. This speaker was famous for her sleep-inducing talks across the borough.

Why can't a staff meeting be a voluntary process? If you want to help with a new initiative or help prepare for the school production, go to them; if not, do something in the school that you find more useful. There is a very old and very worthy proverb that a volunteer is worth ten pressed men: how true! In conclusion to this little section, ask yourself what is better for the children – a gym club or pottery class led by someone who really enjoys their subject, or mind-numbing reams of regurgitated bunkum?

Now let us move on to a little later in your first term.

You are going to have to face the parents of your little protégés at what are sometimes called parents' evenings or, more popular nowadays, 'open days'. The school will be awash with mums and dads, all wanting to hear how little Gillian has fared in her new class. You are very likely to be at a distinct psychological disadvantage in that most of the parents will be a lot older than you. My advice would be to bite the bullet and tell the truth, the whole truth, and nothing but the truth. Ninety-nine times out of a hundred the parents will back you up. Make a few notes about each child and perhaps have samples of their work to hand and lists of their nefarious deeds that you can use to prove a point.

One of the big problems about pretending that idle little George from 4G is not doing too badly is that the parents will commit this to memory for ever, and when it is pointed out in years to come that there is a bit of a problem you will be directly quoted. The chances are that you will have experience of this at your very first meeting. You will find that if you take this up with the teacher concerned they will deny any complicity. One modern trend is to have the children in with their parents to face the music. This usually results in hordes of pupils swarming around the school and driving the caretaker hairless. If the children have to be there, they should be made stay with the parent or be able to sit in a waiting room with lots of spelling tables etc.

During the school year, certain little 'out of the ordinaries' crop up. Visiting theatre groups are a good example, or perhaps a guest speaker in assembly. Many of the schools in my locality availed themselves of the services of the 'The Animal Man'. He took great delight in picking the newest members of staff to help him demonstrate his livestock. I've seen embarrassed NQTs climbing wall bars and being pooped on by pandas. The children loved it (so did the rest of the staff). Anyhow, all these little extras bring a little sunshine to the job and brighten up what would otherwise have been a wet, playtime-less day.

You will probably have to organise a school trip. These are

supposed to be curriculum related, but a little imagination can get around that. For example, a trip to Alton Towers sounds better if is described as 'An educational visit to investigate machines harnessing gravitational potential energy to produce rapid changes in direction and acceleration.' Wherever you go you will have the responsibility of pricing it up, producing risk assessments and extracting the necessary cash from the children. You will now, no doubt, realise the importance of keeping in the secretary's good side!

School sports days used to be one of the highlights of the year, and once again gave the children the chance to see their teachers as actual human beings. Some bright philosopher came up with the idea that children shouldn't be put in a situation where they could lose. This resulted in many schools adopting a 'carousel of activities' sports event. Throwing the health and safety approved sponge, or catching the hypo-allergenic pillow are two examples of these challenges. What's happened to the dads' tug of war or the young mums' 100-metre race? I used to particularly like those.

And, what is more, what's wrong with children losing a race? Surely learning to accept failure or defeat is part of education; we all have to face it at some time in our lives. We always managed to find an event to accommodate all shapes, sizes and abilities of children, and funnily enough the children who came last often got the biggest round of applause. If the powers that be really want our country to excel in world sporting events they will have to realise that attitudes and skills start at grass-roots level in primary schools.

The last and perhaps the most onerous part of the school year is writing reports. Again, my first few years were devoid of them. Since then I've written reports of the 'Mathematics – satisfactory, English – satisfactory, PE – must remember his/her kit' style. Or the open letter variety: 'Dear Mrs Billingsgate, Your charming daughter, Cruella, has excelled in all forms of sport this year and I really think you should have a word with her about it!'

Nowadays the reports have degenerated to the computer word bank system. We were told that this would take the entire grind out of report writing. Rubbish. First you will suffer repetitive stress problems in your right index finger. You will still have to type in a personal comment for each child, making sure that each one is a little different, as parents will compare and contrast. You will then have to download the whole lot into a word processor and edit every single line of every report. Hour upon hour of work, when all that most parents want to hear is that their child is behaving in school, doing their best and hasn't fallen behind. Finally you will print out the entire batch and send them to a member of senior management for checking. Inevitably they will find errors and omissions, and back to the computer you go. Another rainforest destroyed.

Anyway, that's it, you've completed your first year. You have tendered your fond farewells to the children. You've shovelled out the classroom in preparation for the new school year, you're off to the pub, and best of all you are qualified. Not an NQT, or a 'probationer' as it used to be called, but a proper bona fide teacher earning a closer to respectable salary. Now, unless you decide to see sense and take that job at the supermarket, prepare yourself for the future by reading the next chapter.

Policies and planning – a plethora of piffle

'Education,' so thrice uttered Blair,
'Comes first' – however, beware:
For his ideas of quality
Were at odds with reality,
Now it's paper, not children, I fear.

I hate to hark back to the good old days again, but I will try (not promise) to make it the last time.

I was asked why I use the word 'plethora' in the title of this chapter. I was going to use the word pulchritude as there is a certain abstract beauty in the nonsense, but decided on plethora as it didn't spoil the alliteration, and it perhaps describes more clearly the whole nonsensical baggage.

When I started teaching at my first primary school back in 1971, I was given a copy of the school syllabus. Bearing in mind it was a four-year, two-form entry junior school, the entire document occupied no more than four A4 (quarto in those days) sides, not sheets, of paper! We were provided with sets of textbooks for the children and were lucky enough to have an excellent reference library aimed at the children's and teacher's level. Usually schools adopted a school-wide maths and English scheme. True, some of these were better than others, but they gave us a backbone on which we could build and ensured that no vital chunks were missed out. There was of course the usual teacher's book to go with each scheme. With all of this there didn't seem a great deal of point in writing it all out again. One of my favourite schemes was the old Alpha/Beta maths books. ('Boo, hiss!' I hear you say. Never mind. I, and a good many others, found it did the job admirably, and I still use many of its ideas and methods.) Consequently the planning needed could be as basic or as complicated as the individual teacher desired. Some heads would look at planning occasionally – it was something to exchange the newspaper for if an official from the office called by – and sign it at the bottom.

I was not formally asked for any written planning for years. Our planning time could therefore be used to make the curriculum creative and stimulating. Visits, craftwork and art were far less difficult to organise or fit into the timetable. Remember, planning time, especially in primary schools, was in our own time, not part of the school day. Good planning meant being mentally prepared for the topic you were teaching and having a good working knowledge of the subjects involved. Good primary teachers are not just Jacks or Jills of all trades, they are excellent craftsmen. (I have always thought that the term 'craftsman' a better term than professional for teachers, although of course we do the job in a professional way.)

Let's look more closely at what has happened. Planning has in many ways become the altar to which you must all bow down. If you don't you are thrown into the fiery furnace of the PDH's office. I've spent quite some time now as a supply teacher since the first chapter of this little work and have come to the conclusion that Samuel Langhorne Clemens (Mark Twain, if you didn't already know) was absolutely correct. There are lies, damned lies… and planning (no apologies for the substitution). In many schools you are taken to your classroom, sorry, teaching base, and are told in a low reverential tone that the day's planning is on the desk. At first I was naïve enough to be impressed. Not for long!

What is in vogue in many schools today is to produce the planning using the computer on what are fondly known as 'planning grids'. Nine times out of ten they are totally incomprehensible – not just to me but to other supply teachers, learning support staff et al. I believe a strong element of the Emperor's New Clothes syndrome has crept into planning policies: lots to talk about but completely without substance. Let me just quote one example from a school in which I worked. In one literacy lesson I was taking, the planning asked for the children to move to their groups, let's say Bison, Moose, Elephants and Rhinos. I politely requested the children to do this and was met with blank stares. The groups were actually pure fiction which could be twisted into fact in the event of a future Ofsted inspection. (Ofsted inspectors will believe anything that is printed out from a computer – but that's another chapter.) Next, ask the children to get out their 'izzy wizzy, let's get busy' folders. Again, blank stares with muttering of, 'Miss said something about that last September.' Things began to take on an air of surrealism. What was I supposed to be teaching? On further inspection I found that the grid contained little if anything of use. There were references to photocopiable worksheets, OHP resources, National Curriculum attainment targets etc., none of which could be found. I had already discovered that if I pointed this out to a member of senior management (teachers promoted to where they can do less damage), I would get one of a set of stock answers, namely:

'It's probably made clear in medium-term planning.'

'It's probably made clear in long-term planning.'

Or, most popular:

'Planning is under review by senior management at the moment.'

Many new age teachers have computer planning raised to the level of a fine art. Minimalist, perhaps; Cut and Paste-a-list is closer to the truth. If you want to go down this avenue follow these guidelines and you won't go far wrong.

1. Treat your planning grid as a canvas. Don't forget what you write does not matter one iota. The font style, size and colour are crucial.

2. Cut and paste exactly the same text into each cell.

3. Change the colour, font style and size for each cell of your grid.

4. If possible, slap in some clip art. It takes the eye away from the rubbish you have written.

There you have it – designer planning. Not too time-consuming, very pretty and totally useless. If you get any awkward questions from the powers that be, tell them you are trying out a system of differentiation using colour coding. Be careful, they may try to take out copyright on it. A file full of these can look quite attractive, and don't forget, consecutive weeks can be identical. If asked, just say it is follow-up work or reinforcement.

While we are on the subject of planning folders, let us consider the case of 'The Incredible Shrinking Curriculum'. At the birth of the National Curriculum a couple of decades ago, every state primary school teacher in the country was presented with a set of folders, one for each subject. (Another interesting fact is that these documents were published at about the same time as the consultation documents were issued – fait accompli, peut-être?) It is rumoured that this cost the taxpayer in the region of £800 million… say it slowly: *zero point eight billion pounds per person*. My double A4 sheet would cost about 10p, including ink. Within a very short time it was scrapped (not the term used by the authorities) and a slimmer version of four or five folders per teacher was produced; which was within a very short time, you've guessed it, scrapped. The next version consisted of one paperback volume occupying a tiny fraction of the shelf space of the first edition. If the authors of these documents continue nibbling, the correct side of the cake perhaps it will vanish completely! I could go along the evolutionary pathway and chat about numeracy and literacy strategies but not just at the moment, perhaps in another chapter.

Let's move on to policies and, as it happens, strangely enough, stockrooms. Not so many years ago, stockrooms were little gold mines of resources. Card, paper, paints and brushes; jealously guarded scissors and rulers, carefully labelled and numbered, just in case Miss Jones from next door attempted to purloin them. Stockrooms were very much a reflection of their owner. My very first one contained a huge papier mâché model, covered in green bottle tops, of what I first thought was a crocodile. It turned out that the previous owner was a J R R Tolkien fan and the model was Smaug, the dragon from *The Hobbit*. Another teacher had a room carefully filled with stacks of crisp boxes, all containing identical heaps of junk. They were carefully labelled 'resources for art' or 'resources for design technology' etc. and all contained, among other things, identical heaps of empty margarine tubs, washing-up liquid bottles and yoghurt pots. The computer and its trolley were known affectionately by the rest of the staff as 'the crisp box stand'. I believe that when the teacher left the contents of the room were moved, as one job lot, into an industrial skip.

Look into any stockroom now, in virtually any school in the country, and you will see exactly the same thing. Shelves full of policy documents, out of date schemes of work and the odd faded copy of the previous version of the National Curriculum. All gathering dust and untouched by human hand for years.

I always thought that policies were things the government produced and nobody understood. In that I am at least partly right, the difference being that now everybody has them. Nowadays there has to be a policy document for every conceivable subject and situation. Just ask to see all the schools' current policies. Storing them would stretch the facilities of the British Library. What do policies actually do? With the excessive interest Ofsted has in them, probably very little. Everybody, however, seems very concerned that they are all in place. Precisely what place I'm not sure; possibly threaded onto a piece of string in a private (and very small) office.

Now, a few little bits of jargon with which you need to be acquainted. First, IEPs, (Individual Education Plans). These first appeared under the umbrella of Special Educational Needs, SEN. They were produced by the Special Needs Coordinator, the SENCO, to help children struggling with different aspects of the curriculum. Don't expect to have any input, as many SENCOs consider themselves all-seeing and all-knowing. The government has come up with the wonderful idea that perhaps all children should have an IEP, as all children are different. Good God, they are quick, aren't they! Where they think the time will be found to produce the things I have no idea. I doubt very much if you will understand one word that is in an IEP, as they will be filled with terms such as targets, objectives and outcomes and will almost certainly have been produced on the computer in the ubiquitous grid format.

And now to what I consider one of the greatest cans of worms. *Assessment!*

In Chapter 1, the Prologue, I pointed out that children are being tested from the cradle to the grave.

'Yes,' they say, 'but we have to know what level the children have reached.'

Poppycock! Levels tell you absolutely nothing that you could not have observed in the ordinary day-to-day running of the class. A good teacher is assessing continually by talking and listening to children, observing their work and more importantly the social skills and attitudes they are developing. What is the point of formal assessment unless you go back and put right those areas in which achievement is low? You can't do this, as you are compelled to move on regardless of the results.

You have to have the dreaded evidence of assessment much the same as for planning.

Some pointers. Photocopy bits of children's work, it doesn't necessarily have to be from your school. Formally level the work and finally have it countersigned by someone, preferably a close relative on your mother's side. You can then use this as evidence that all your children's work is rigorously assessed. You don't have to have the names of the children on the work but a little black rectangle of sugar paper when photocopying will make it quite clear that you are hiding the child's identity for reasons of security – the little touches make all the difference.

Graphical displays of data can be very impressive. A standard class list on a grid filled with numbers randomly inserted is useful. Give the same grid different headings and you can halve your work. Scatter graphs are wonderful, especially if you use the toothbrush method. Good quality graph paper is an essential. Label the axis with real educational terms arranged in an incomprehensible order. For example, 'A graphical analysis of the effect of reading recoverability on the transient, undiagnosed dyslexic.' Then pick up the toothbrush. Dip it into some ready prepared paint or ink. Stand a little under half a metre from the paper – and flick! With practice you can produce normal curves, skewed curves, results showing correlation or not. Two colour spraying can show change over time. The possibilities are endless.

I'm afraid I can't finish this chapter without mentioning the greatest immorality of all, KS2 SATs. It appears that in the majority of primary schools education is put on hold in year six and is replaced by never ending coaching in the core subjects. For what? They are of absolutely no benefit whatsoever to the children – quite the contrary, in fact. They are not, on the whole, used by secondary schools when setting children, and they result in totally demoralised children who think they have failed because they haven't reached their predicted level. Because of the importance of a school's position on the ubiquitous league tables, however, some heads will go to extraordinary lengths to get good results. In one school where I had worked for a considerable number of years, two children had been absent from school the first part of SATs week. They were very bright children, dead certainties for a top level. The head actually gave them the test papers to do when they arrived back to school and made sure that their absence was not on record. Would that head have done the same for struggling Craig? I think not.

SATs do not just affect the year six children who are taking them. Every member of staff, including those from administration, will be called on to act as readers, amanuenses and givers out of paper and pencils. All of a sudden their importance in other areas of the school fades into insignificance. The school also takes on the feel of a mortuary. People walk around the school on tiptoe and talk in subdued whispers. Sad!

Packs of examination papers can be opened an hour before the test is due to take place. This is supposedly to check that the correct numbers of copies are present and there are no errors in the printing. It would, however, be most interesting to find how many schools have last minute spelling or science lessons an hour before this test!

One of the greatest dangers of this system is that children are pushed to unrealistic levels that they cannot maintain at secondary school. I have a number of private pupils whose parents are really worried because the levels their children achieved at primary school have actually gone *down*. This in fact happened with my own children. If they were still of primary school age I would withdraw them from school during SATs week. Despite what the government says, parents are entitled to take children on holiday in school term time. Wouldn't it be wonderful if everyone followed this example. It could result in a completely horizontal league table: wonderful!

The amount of time spent on all levels of assessment is

beyond belief. I was truly shocked to go into a school in January and find the hall set out for the year six pupils to do practice SAT papers. This was in a school that I thought had more sense. In a strange way it is almost understandable. A fall in your overall test results cause you to go down on that other piece of immorality, The League Table. This in turn brings on the likelihood of an inspection. When is anything taught? Seemingly in the diminishing times between assessments. The vast majority of heads see the futility of this nonsense, which brings me to the last question of this chapter. Why don't they all stand together and say, 'No, this is wrong. We want to educate children, not demoralise them.'

Fortunately this seems to be the stance that is being taken by the Head Teacher Association and other teacher unions at their respective annual conferences. A touch of sanity on the horizon, perhaps?

I am not a technophobe!

The gadgets that once were a must
Have vanished neath layers of dust.
So watch out, what they flog
In Galt's catalogue
Are gizmos – it's you that comes fust!

I repeat, I am not a technophobe. I am rapidly coming to the conclusion however, that the very best place for about ninety per cent of primary school and very likely secondary school computers would be a large skip in the school playground!

They can be very useful educational tools but unfortunately they are being used not as tools, but as teachers, which they most emphatically are not. Saying that, I have lost count of the times I have seen classes or groups of children marched down to the computer suite (usually cramped, stuffy and windowless) told to log on to 'education am us.com', click on programme 3, Part 2, section 1, paragraph b, and get on with it.

If you make the mistake of questioning the educational value of this you usually get the reply, 'We have to do this because it's our allocated computer suite time.' I am under the impression it is officially allocated time-killing time!

I have to agree that the use of the information and display capabilities of computers can be an important element of class topic, but on the whole I do not think this is how they are being used. Children spend a large amount of their own time glued in front of television screens, PlayStations, Xboxes etc. They come to school and what do we do? We shove them in front of screens!

Anyway, for the moment, let's get away from computers and move on to more basic technology.

In the natural world, when a creature has evolved to the optimum design for its environment it stops evolving. That supreme example of marine life, the shark, has remained unchanged for millions of years. If only the same could be true in the classroom. Let's consider a glaring example, 'the Blackboard', perfectly designed, inexpensive, long-lasting and easy to maintain. Its main accessory, chalk, is very cheap, available in a multitude of colours and with its partner, the board rubber, made excellent missiles for maintaining discipline. There were one or two varieties of the basic model, roller boards for example, but for years it reigned supreme. Children in early days even had their own mini-boards and chalks.

It was too good to last.

First the name changed. For reasons of political correctness it had to be called the 'the Chalkboard' – ridiculous! Some were even green in colour (let's hear it for the Martians). Then along came 'the Whiteboard' (why, for the sake of the same political correctness is this not called 'the Inkboard'?) The pens are expensive, run out quickly, and if the top is left off for more than five minutes they dry up beyond recovery. Some of the pens were solvent-based and could leave you in a state of euphoria after prolonged use. Others were water-based and the board had to be cleaned with a damp cloth, and others were dry wiped. The worst case scenario with these boards occurred if you inadvertently picked up a permanent marker and filled the entire board with writing. It could take hours to clean away the offending debris.

However, worse was to come, 'The Smart Board' appeared and from then on all hell broke loose. These wonderful machines, linked to the computer network, would provide all that was needed to teach. Wrong! They are incredibly clever pieces of equipment and can be of enormous benefit but once again they are being used for purposes for which they were not designed. They don't, for example, replace a decent surface for writing on or a decent tool to write with. If you examine these smart (and expensive) pens in a school that has had them for some time you will see the ends are gradually wearing away.

Different models of these boards work in slightly different ways. This is very confusing for a supply teacher. On some boards if you pick up two pens at once the board starts to sulk, or if you leave a blue pen out an inadvertent flick of the finger leaves a dirty azure streak across the screen.

One thing guaranteed to raise my blood pressure is when you start writing with the magic pen and your script appears, as if by a miracle, half a metre away.

'Please sir, the board needs recalibrating, sir. Can I do it, sir? Please sir…'

You know, I've never known a piece of chalk that needed recalibrating, or for that matter cause quite such disruption. Horses for courses. Yes, use Smart Boards, but don't sling out the older, but still useful, technology.

There is a current theory that the demise of the world's rain-forests is caused by slash-and-burn farming and global warming. I personally think that they began to diminish with the advent of the photocopier, or at least a photocopier cheap enough for schools to use. The budget for the paper used by educational establishments has rocketed. At a recent staff meeting I attended, the headmaster showed a little concern that half a million sheets of best printing paper had been used during one term. It appeared to have disappeared into the black hole of stationery, as there was no evidence of this paper on display or in children's folders. Whole stockrooms are dedicated to storing paper of every hue. For what purpose? To produce reams upon reams of worksheets, which at the end of the school year end up in the bin, or at best are recycled? I have seen teachers draw a freehand circle on a piece of paper and then make thirty copies of it. Looking at many such copies I have come to the conclusion that it would be far wiser to take an unopened pack of paper and sling it straight into the recycling bin.

Originally, copying was in the hand of the school head or secretary and the machine used was a hand-cranked Gestetner (ink copier). These were notoriously temperamental and would cover the user in a layer of printer's ink at the slightest provoca-tion. Staff were allowed to use the spirit duplicator. There were certain advantages to this because of the nature of the spirit used. Ten minutes in the copying room would leave the user in a state of fume-induced euphoria which would have cost a fortune to achieve in a public house. Looking back, I can see why certain teachers would offer to do your copying. They were the ones who didn't appear to have a care in the world and drifted from lesson to lesson, smiling beatifically. Because these machines were somewhat difficult to use and great care had to be taken over the production of your master copy, printing was kept to the essentials.

So far, schools couldn't actually copy an existing document or picture. If you really needed this you would have to avail yourself of a copying or printing service. Then along came the heat copier. In a long and involved procedure you could produce a copy (black and white only) of a single-sheet document. If you wanted a picture from a page in a book you could forget it unless you were prepared to tear the page out. The copy made was on a flimsy sheet of special paper and in a short time if left in the open would fade. In hindsight, these machines didn't have a great deal of impact although, at the time, we thought they were wonderful.

Now every school has a state-of-the-art copier and printer and can produce copies, legal and otherwise, at a rate of thousands per hour. The legal situation is extremely confusing. You are allowed to copy certain sections from some books without charge and can pay for the right to copy other material. Some books are freely photocopiable and others not. Don't get caught even *looking* at a photocopy of music; transportation could ensue! Having said this, show me the person who has not used an illegal photocopy and I'll show you the next candidate for canonisation.

My big argument with photocopies is that yet again they are being used for purposes they were not intended. Why give complex worksheets when children are quite capable of reading charts, books, question sheets and then producing their own written work in quality exercise books? Surely only best copies for display should be written on individual sheets of paper.

Another, I believe, huge problem in using copied sheets is that (theoretically) they all have to be stored, usually in some expensive file or envelope. I know that many of them are simply filed away in that wonderful wire mesh storage system by the classroom door – what a waste!

Before I get on to my pet dislike, the pc, here is just a simple list of some of the technical innovations that have appeared and rapidly disappeared from the equipment cupboard.

The Epidiascope

An extremely complicated (and expensive) optical machine that used a complex arrangement of mirrors and lenses to project a picture from any book onto a screen.

DISADVANTAGES: the room had to be blacked out completely to get an image you could see. Goodness knows what was going on on the back row.

STATUS QUO: museum pieces, although many of the lenses were filched by the physics department.

The Synchrofax

A cross between a magnetic recorder and work card. You could buy mass-produced resources, often popular with teachers of younger children.

DISADVANTAGES: blank work cards were expensive and tricky to prepare.

STATUS QUO: museum pieces, although I have recently seen a couple gathering dust on a remote stockroom shelf.

The Video Camera

A difficult one this. It is one of those machines that have gone through many incarnations, usually getting cheaper at each stage. I feel really sorry for parent associations who worked to raise a thousand pound to buy a state-of-the-art VHS video camera only to find it obsolete within a couple of years. I took one of these machines to school camp and have a wonderful piece of film, about one hour long, of turf with occasional flashes of sky – they're not the easiest things to use. It is possible to trace the family history of this equipment from cine film all the way through to cheap, hand-held digital cameras.

STATUS QUO: because of the current mania for evidence the genre is still thriving.

The list could go on. Slide projectors, film strip projectors, reel-to-reel tape recorders, cassette recorders, a multitude of mathematical and scientific educational gadgets, even the humble radio and television, once a classroom mainstay. Now all are gone, lost, and never called me mother! Nationwide, millions of pounds worth of scrap.

Now back to my favourite moan, the computer.

I am the first to admit that they are a fantastic piece of equipment and open the doors to an almost infinite range of resources. The question is still there, however, do they, or will they replace teachers? At the moment I would almost certainly say no. However, I was speaking to a younger colleague who is an ICT coordinator. He believes that in his career children will be set the majority of work online, do it at home and only come to school for the social bits, physical education and counselling etc. I find this absolutely frightening. First, who will do this work? The parents, older brothers and sisters, or even perhaps another computer program?

Much educational software gives children multiple choice questions. Children can sit at the machine and keep guessing until they achieve their 100 per cent score. Does this mean that the children have actually learned anything? Of course it doesn't, but there is a grave danger that wrong concepts will have been hammered into place. One well-known science program I have seen actually told the children that bumblebees were important agents of seed dispersal! I think not.

Computers, it's true, are a fantastic source of up-to-the-minute information that can be accessed at the touch of the button and printed out with equal ease. If children used this information source correctly I would be 100 per cent behind the machines. This often does not happen. Let's look at an example. 5G are doing a topic on European countries, and Bill goes home and carries out a search on Croatia on his dad's computer. If the work was then read carefully, the relevant bits copied and pasted everything would be fine. Nine times out of ten, though, Bill will press the print button and produce thirty sheets of what to him will be incomprehensible jargon. There is a fair chance as well that the whole thing will be written in Croatian, as that will be the first site that he clicked on. There is also the very real danger that at home Bill will find some of the less savoury material provided by the World Wide Web. Schools usually screen out any material that is in the least bit dubious. I doubt very much if dad's computer has the same facility.

Computers are with us and I can't see them vanishing from schools, but I personally feel teachers are becoming far too reliant on them.

Inspection! Stand by your kits

There was once an inspector called Lars
Whose knowledge of teaching was sparse
He thought that Piaget
Was a scent by Fabergé
And Patrick Moore penned *Life on Mars*

Those of you who were readers of the *Beano* will no doubt remember the Bash Street Kids: Cuthbert, Smiffy, Wilfred, Plug, Danny and of course Teacher. Teacher's only real fear was the arrival of the government inspector. Everyone rallied round against the common enemy, even the normally roguish class members.

Inspectors of that era were doubtlessly feared but everyone was aware that the inspectors had once been teachers themselves and to achieve the status of HMI (Her Majesty's Inspector) they had to be good. My goodness, times have changed.

One level below these icons were the local authority inspectors/advisors. The title changed depending on which political power led the council. Some of these were good; others, as is often the case, had been promoted to where they could do less damage. On a slightly lower level were the advisory teachers. There was often a seasonal flush of these when a school had to be closed. Rather than make teachers redundant, a bad political move, they were moved to the teachers' centre, and ran courses on the use of glue sticks (a modern innovation) and pond dipping (without a pond, of course, for health and safety reasons).

Schools nowadays have their own systems of internal inspection under the general heading of 'Monitoring of Teaching and Learning', a government idea to promote improvement in standards. Remember the Prologue? One would think, at first sight, that this wasn't such a bad idea, but I keep on having visions of grannies and eggs being sucked. I vaguely object (I can't be bothered to strongly object to anything nowadays) to a twenty-something teacher telling me that I haven't put my LO (Learning Objective) on the board, or perhaps that the children haven't written down their WALT (What we Are Learning Today). I have always worked on the principle that the children should be able to tell you at the end of the lesson what they have or haven't learned. Slower children will spend the whole lesson writing down the date and the WALT and will, from an educational point of view, have achieved essentially nothing. New teaching ideas are not necessarily good just because of the fact that they are new or have come from QCA (The Qualifications and Curriculum Authority) or Ofsted.

Ah! Ofsted, the Office for Standards in Education. What a misnomer!

What exactly is this creature? About two decades ago it was introduced, along with the National Curriculum, to improve what were deemed as lowering standards. The National Curriculum provided the means, and Ofsted the policing, of the whole shebang. Failing schools would be weeded out and entire staff would be replaced by 'experts'. Schools would be 'turned around' and inner city academies would flood Oxford and Cambridge with eager students…

Now why, you ask, do we need this when we already have HMI to do the job. The answer is in the acronym HMI, Her Majesty's Inspectors. They were not directly answerable to the government and could comment on things that were not put into Ofsted's brief – conditions of school buildings and educational funding, for example. This was in addition to their job of inspecting teachers. They could therefore cause great embarrassment to the government in power at the time. Nowadays HMIs are only brought in after Ofsted has finished its dirty work to officiate over improvements.

Who exactly are these new inspectors? Ninety-five per cent of HMIs are qualified and experienced teachers, often with further experience at Local Education Authority level. Ofsted inspectors are usually nothing of the sort. It is possible to become one without having a breath of educational experience. It took three years of training and more years than I care to mention to become an adequately proficient teacher. (Modesty forbids me going any further than this.) If you wish you can become an Ofsted inspector in not much more than a couple of weeks. You do not need to have an IQ of much more than average, if that. You need to be able to fill in a tick chart and be good at pretending you know what you are talking about. You will not have to do a great deal of writing, as the major part of the report will be assembled from banks of statements on your laptop. This also explains why reports all look essentially the same. You need to be able to scan the masses of paperwork the school will have provided and decide whether it is up to scratch. What you most certainly do not have to do is to make comments such as, 'My God, these teachers are doing a bloody good job in very difficult circumstances.' Remarks like that could turn you into a HMI and hence struck off the Ofsted register.

What sort of people do become inspectors? A large proportion of them are retired teachers, in fact people who should know better. A former head teacher with whom I worked for a number of years was always scathing about them until he realised what a nice little earner it was. He then made the mistake of bragging that he had become 'a Qualified Inspector'. I do not know if he was expecting congratulations, pats on the back etc. I had never really liked the bloke but I, and a great many others, had great difficulty in being polite to him again. The fact of the matter is however that it does pay well, doesn't take up too much time and you can walk away afterwards, no matter what harm or good you have done.

If you teach in a Church of England school you might find yourself lumbered with an inspector from your diocese. I had one of these, a lady who was deeply concerned about the spirituality of the school. Please, oh please, what did she mean? When asked, I mouthed a few sentences of nonsense and we were therefore given a 'good' in that area. The same lady, out of the kindness of her heart, came to the school and gave my class a demonstration dance lesson. The children, bless 'em, didn't riot. Myself, and the classroom assistant, who happened to be a very good qualified dance teacher, stood back and watched in disbelief. If I had produced the same lesson I would have been slated without mercy.

The nature of the inspections has changed a good deal over the years, mainly because enough people won't take on the job. I don't really blame them for that. When they first appeared schools were given up to six months' notice. This meant that for a long period of time teachers were working themselves into a state of total mental collapse. Policies were polished (or not), planning was perfected and classrooms de-cluttered. The LEA would send in the troops and give the school a mock inspection. These were usually more traumatic than the real thing. The inspection itself lasted 4½ days and you were guaranteed to be seen at least four or five times. The team was introduced to the staff on the morning of the first day. Paraded, in fact, like the final round of a Miss World competition. The Friday afternoon was reserved for feedback to 'de management'. Each teacher was then given a sealed brown paper envelope with the results of their personal lesson inspections. One school that I knew of had a ceremonial binning of the unopened envelopes at four thirty on the Friday. The head teacher who led this was in fact an ex-LEA advisor who had gone back to the chalk face after being told that he would have to undergo Ofsted training. Good for him; I wish there had been a few more of his ilk.

Because of the lack of inspectors, the visits dwindled until they now last just a couple of days, and if you 'do well' you are excused them for a number of years. If you don't the circling HMIs will descend to the feast.

How to get through an inspection with as few problems as possible? This is actually easier than it sounds. Don't forget that, on the whole, inspectors are not gifted with great intelligence and hence easily manipulated. The policies, planning and associated piffle is usually well up to date in most schools, mainly thanks to the fact that the senior management seem to do little else in their spare time. Make sure your own planning and record files are up to date, perhaps following my suggestions from a previous chapter. It is well worth while to produce a more detailed plan for each individual lesson likely to be seen. If they are reading this they can't be watching you so closely; and always remember to have plenty of backup material for those children who will finish the set task in thirty seconds.

There is always the problem of the one group of children I mentioned previously. Remember, those who have their 'little problems'. They are hard enough to deal with at the best of times but you can guarantee that when an inspector, or for that matter any visitor, is present they will surpass themselves. A method of dealing with the situation used by some schools is to board them out at another school for the week under the pretext that the children are, for example, researching a topic that that school actually specialises in. Recommending a severe illness that lasts about a week sometimes works, but for this you would need parental cooperation, often not forthcoming in these cases. If all else fails, send them, with their minder, to some remote corner of the school to produce artwork, or carry out a traffic survey, or tidy out the PE/art cupboard.

The overall physical impression of the classroom environment is quite, but not critically important. Have a healthy balance of children's artwork and handwritten texts, combined with displays of mathematical and English instructional material. Graphs and house points lists add to the overall effect. A few models with bits that move will clinch it. Remember, children are really not in the least bit interested in what is on the four walls, they're more concerned in getting out of them. There may be the odd flash of interest when they see a piece of their own work that they can brag about to their parents. Likewise, Ofsted will show a cursory interest. If it looks good at slightly more than a passing glance you've won.

During my last but one inspection I prepared every single lesson meticulously – apart from a twenty-minute PSHE session (Personal, Social and Health Education, for the uninitiated). What happened? Fifteen minutes before the official start time of this lesson there was a knock at the door and a timid little face appeared. 'Please could I watch your PSHE lesson?' Unusually good manners for one of their ilk, I thought. The children had the class cleared in record-breaking time. I carefully wrote the words 'Moral Dilemma' on the board and recited, from memory, 'Matilda told such dreadful lies...'

The class were wonderful and we had an enlightening discussion of the rights and wrong of telling lies. The inspector said thank you and she disappeared the way she had come. The head teacher confided to me later that the inspector thought that this was one of the best PSHE lessons she had observed. I thanked him and said nothing. *But*, don't forget, I was experienced and I was very lucky. It doesn't take a lot of time to prepare a couple of days' worth of lessons, so make sure you prepare them all.

One thing that I find extremely annoying is the lack of respect that is often shown for the school's normal daily routine. During my last inspection an inspector came to watch the school assembly. A lot of effort had gone into making it a little special. Children were making music, awards were being presented, and of course it was also an act of worship. I am not, with the wildest stretch of the imagination, a religious person, but I found it difficult to swallow the lack of respect and manners shown by the inspector who, after scribbling copious notes, walked out halfway through.

Whatever you do during an inspection, never say there is anything wrong or even slightly below par in the school. Everything is wonderful; the management are truly fantastic, relationships between staff, pupils and parents are great, and really you couldn't have picked a better school in which to begin your career. If you have any worries or misgivings, keep them to yourself. If there is anything detrimental to the school that could be found out, let them find it; they probably won't. Don't forget the head and senior staff will have virtually written the report. All Ofsted do is rubber stamp it.

Bandwagons, quangos and other curious quirks

PPA, KS2, SAT
QCA, SEN, NQT:
In acronym sounds
The profession abounds –
LEA, HMI, AST.

In every single trade or profession, wonderful new ideas and innovations appear that are hailed as world changing. These are copied, modified and adopted by myriads of different groups and then, like the Cheshire cat in *Alice in Wonderland*, they gradually fade away, leaving behind only the smirk of the people who are likely to have made a fortune from them. This little chapter will attempt to introduce you to a few of the ones currently found in schools, and also a few of those that have disappeared into that great educational glory hole in the sky.

First, to the quangos, or perhaps one should say 'The Quango'.

Teachers were at one time represented at a professional level by their unions and by their LEAs. The powers that be in government circles upon high weren't too keen on this idea at all. Unions of course are disliked by all politicians, regardless of their political leanings, and LEAs on the other hand were often at odds with the current parliamentary colour. So what did they do? They came up with the brilliant idea of creating 'The General Teaching Council for England'. The leaders of this organisation would be in overall charge of disciplinary matters. Teachers who were struck from the membership would be unable to work in schools in England or Wales. The idea basically was to put teaching on a similar professional footing as doctors and nurses.

The truth of the matter is the GTC is regarded with hostility by a large percentage of the teaching profession. We were put on the list, given a pretty piece of plastic with our registration number, and then charged £33 a year for the privilege. In return we get countless sheets of questionnaires and photographs of the happy smiling team. They appear to be what could be described as a school council for grown-ups, (there seems to be a certain pride in this dubious status, something akin to bragging that you are an inspector). A newsletter occasionally drops on the mat telling us what a wonderful contribution they are making to staffroom discussion. The only discussions I have heard about the GTC in many staffrooms is unprintable, and in the rest there is no mention at all. There was a minor revolt at the outset about teachers having to cough up money for an organisation that they didn't want. To counter this, the government came up with wonderful idea of giving teachers £33 each, with which they could pay their membership fee. Let's cut out the middleman, eh! I wonder, do we actually pay income tax on this cash? I wouldn't be at all surprised.

On my last newsletter/dues reminder they congratulated themselves on keeping the membership fee the same for the nth year in a row, thus saving teachers money. I could quite easily save teachers and the government exactly £33 a year. At the moment, you will have to get signed up to full membership. There is one strange advantage. The membership number on your little piece of plastic is the same as your superannuation number, often asked for on job application forms. It is, also, very useful when going for early retirement, and is not too easily lost.

There have been numerous subject bandwagons on which to hitch a ride, far too many, in fact, to be listed here. Here's just a few just to give you a little taster.

Many years ago, when I was studying for my degree with the Open University, I had an interesting conversation with a fellow student. He had his career clearly mapped out.

'Safety is the flavour of the year,' he said. 'Mark my words, my boy, there are going to be some very good jobs in this area.'

We all howled down the idea as being quite ludicrous. He was proved, however, to be quite correct. The amount of paperwork generated by the dictates of the Health and Safety Executive almost surpasses that required for planning and assessment. A lot of this palaver was caused by some leaders on school visits and adventure-type holidays making thoughtless decisions, sometimes with tragic results. The HSE themselves are not entirely to blame for some of the ridiculous safety rules employed in some schools – the banning of games of conkers, for example. The outcome, though, has had far-reaching effects on many school activities, especially in the area of school trips.

Nowadays no visit can be made without the completion of a formal risk assessment document. These take a considerable amount of time to produce, and I am afraid to say are often considered as an onerous task and not an important part of your responsibility of care. Risk assessment, however, is not just a paper task. When leading visits one should always be aware of any inherent risks and take measures to reduce them. This may mean going on a pre-visit visit to the area to assess any likely problems. Good teachers and leaders have always done this. It is not what is written down that makes a visit run safely and smoothly. It is what is ingrained in the leader's outlook and their ability to communicate with the individuals under their care. By their very definition accidents will always happen, and it is the duty of every person to learn from them to make all activities safer, not just the HSE.

Now, on quite a different note.

At the beginning of my career you were expected to hear every child in your class read. Despite arguments that the children were just 'barking at words' this did seem to have a positive effect. Then some bright spark came up with the idea of reading mums. Mothers were encouraged to come into schools on a voluntary basis to listen to children read. Teaching unions were opposed to this at the outset, quite rightly saying that mums weren't teachers but were being asked to do a teacher's job. This, they claimed, was the thin end of the wedge. Hindsight has proved them quite correct. Reading mums went through a process of evolution. One of the first species to occur was *Homo sapiens classroomassistensis* – now commonly known as Teaching Assistants or TAs. I wouldn't for a moment suggest that they were the thick end of the wedge that the union predicted, but the fact is that many of them are now expected to do exactly the same job as a teacher for a considerably lower salary. Many of them are extremely good and are, in fact, quiet capable of doing a teacher's job. The reality is however that they are being used as teachers on the cheap.

One thing that I find personally annoying is that supply cover, once the domain of the qualified teacher, is now being provided by TAs. I was chatting to a colleague, a high-level teaching assistant about this. She told me a lovely little anecdote about when a head teacher was showing a group of interviewees around the school. She came into the room and Miss Smith, the HLTA, was introduced with the words, 'This is Mrs Smith, She does everything a teacher does but doesn't get paid as much.' The head teacher then breezed off down the corridor with her entourage.

If they are as good as a teacher they should be given the same salary or actively encouraged to get fully qualified. This is, unfortunately, a luxury that many of them cannot afford. One thing that I have found difficult to get used to are the flocks of TAs that appear when you are trying to teach. On one occasion there was myself and five other adults in the room. Fair enough, each of them had responsibilities. One was a minder for a child with physical problems. Another had care of a pupil 'who had his little learning difficulties', and the rest were in charge of groups. Inevitably the level of noise in the classroom made it difficult to teach, or for that matter, for children to learn. Perhaps we shouldn't go back to the time when you went into your classroom on 1 September and re-emerged on about 18 July without seeing a soul, but perhaps a happy medium could be reached.

As well as the explosion of extra teaching staff in schools, whether qualified or not, there has been a burgeoning of administration staff. In my first school we had a part-time secretary. I believe she worked four mornings a week, and that was it. Her role was to do the dinner numbers, type the odd letter for the head, and lend a sympathetic ear to the moans of the rest of the staff. There are now so many admin staff that many schools appoint an office manager. Of course, along with this comes the inevitable rash of new titles e.g. Learning Link Worker, Community Liaison Officer. The list goes on.

Now, the nine to thirteen science project. The idea behind this scheme was to let children discover science by exploration and investigation. Not a bad idea at first sight. Personally, I prefer the children to discover what I want them to. The project was accompanied by a set of very glossy, very expensive books. There were many very good ideas in the whole scheme but it was extremely difficult to organise, required a large variety of resources, and eventually faded away into obscurity. There are still a few of the books lying around in stock cupboards. They are worth having a look at just for the sake of the quaint photographs of children 'learning'.

Successive governments often had pangs of conscience about the state of foreign language teaching. Local authorities invested huge sums of money in schemes such as '*En Avant*' (a French teaching scheme, believe it or not). Further expense was used training teachers and paying, you've guessed it, specialist advisors, to pop round the schools giving aid and assistance. The scheme eventually vanished, leaving behind boxes of fluffy felt '*animaux et légumes*' and collections of cassettes. Anyway, governmental rumblings seem to indicate that the topic is rearing its ugly head again so beware.

Another curious quirk was as a direct result of the introduction of the National Curriculum and Standard Assessment Tests. In the prologue I christened these 'The National Recipe for Mediocrity'. It catered for the average and just above average, that is all those children who would get level four or five. Children who were less able were also given, eventually, a great deal of help and support. However, a significant group of children were for quite a while totally ignored. These were the ones for who level four or five was a piece of cake. They included children who could read fluently before they started school and for whom basic number work just seemed common sense. I am afraid to say that a number of schools collectively rubbed their hands together at the thought of a few level fives safely in the bag. Very bright children didn't have special needs, and therefore didn't need any extra help!

After a good deal of moaning from certain quarters, the powers that be decided that this was a matter that should be looked at resulting in 'The Gifted and Talented Project'. Of course, there was the usual knee-jerk response. Letters from the school's special needs department were sent to the class teachers requesting a list of all their gifted and talented children. I sent back a careful prepared list containing no names whatsoever. Personally I feel that gifted and talented goes beyond the level of your ordinary bright child, and that if you see a handful of them in your career you have been blessed (or cursed, as they can be extremely hard work).

The project has, however, brought subjects such as art and music into the spotlight that otherwise have been treated in a rather cavalier fashion. I have had the occasional musician or artist who has been outstanding, and more rarely the precocious mathematician or writer. Every year we hear reported the latest prodigy who achieved GCSE maths shortly after arriving home from the maternity hospital. Doesn't this raise that awkward little question, why? One school that I thought had the right idea placed a large poster in their foyer stating, 'All our children are gifted and talented'. God bless them; we should all strive to achieve that attitude.

Some bandwagons actually do seem to work. Fairly recent initiatives such as the Numeracy Project do seem to have a positive impact in the classroom, and I must say that most of the teachers who led the training really seemed to know their stuff. It is a pity that this can't be said of all areas of the curriculum.

While we are on the subject of training it's worth spending a bit of time about that quirky phenomenon that came about because of a rather curious anomaly, that is, the Training Day. Twenty or so years ago, if your school was used as a polling station the children and staff were given the day off. In a good year this could add up to a respectable number of extra days. I remember one particular year when there were council elections, a general election, European elections and a referendum. Unfortunately the school in which I worked was not used as a polling station, so for me it was business as usual. In the middle of the 1980s the current Minister of Education decided that enough was enough, and teachers shouldn't have these bonus days as they already had far too many holidays! (A vaguely hypocritical view, when you consider the empty seats on display at Westminster during a normal working day. Of course, all the MPs will be at work in their constituencies – or their second jobs!)

Days such as these were therefore deemed to be 'training days', and for a considerable number of years were named, in honour of their founder, Baker Days. I changed school at about this time, and had the advantage of just one election day before the axe came down. The upshot of it all was that Baker Days became statutory, and all schools had to build in three days of staff training into each year. Enlightened head teachers try to make them as painless as possible. Little devices such as 'early starts' and 'shorter coffee breaks' can usually be applied so that the day can finish about lunchtime. For PDHs, however, they provide a host of wonderful power-wielding opportunities.

The day is timetabled to the point of submission. Breaks for coffee, lunch and the calls of nature are given grudgingly, and any suggestion that the day might finish a little earlier will draw looks suggesting dismissal for gross misconduct.

The timetable is predictable:

9.00–9.15:	Coffee and welcome
9.15–10.30:	Meet in phase groups to discuss the matters which had nearly driven the phase coordinator suicidal at a previous middle-management meeting.

'Phase group' is another little term that has crept in through the back door. It used to be infants and juniors. Now we have foundation level, middle phase, upper middle phase, lower upper phase, upper lower middle phase etc., etc. Why?

10.30–10.45:	Coffee
10.45–12.15 p.m.	Split into groups to discuss the possibility of life after education.

These little sessions can be fairly entertaining if handled properly. You will probably be given a huge sheet of white paper and an array of felt-tip pens to brainstorm the ideas from your group. It's a great time to be exercising your skills in inventing words and phrases. For example carefully write 'Pedagogical Hetero-gyronomy' in the middle of your sheet. PDH will nod knowingly and make a mental note to check it on the Internet. (Again elements of the Emperor's New Clothes creeping in.) All the groups' sheets will be invariably Blu-tacked around the staffroom and left for several weeks to demonstrate to all school visitors what a fruitful time the whole day was.

12.15–1.00 p.m.:	Lunch
1.00–3.00 p.m.:	Guest speaker. (If you should start warming to one of these characters, just bear in mind they are getting paid a lot more than you are for doing the same talk week after week.)
3.00 p.m.:	Plenary. Where do we go from here? (If you have any sense, the pub.)

Another little quirk that has crept into schools over the last few years is PPA time, i.e. preparation, planning and assessment. In the good old days, planning was carried out in your own time. Quite rightly, however, the realisation has dawned that the amount of claptrap that has to be produced by the chalk face teacher cannot be done in the few available hours left outside school time. Teachers have therefore been granted ten per cent of their time as free for paperwork. Great news from a supply teacher's point of view, it has, as have outbreaks of gastro-enteritis, influenza and pregnancy, provided me with quite a fair income over the last couple of years. The fact is however the taxpayer is again forking out large sums of money – totally unnecessarily, in many people's opinion.

What's in a name? Looking at the current craze for changing school names, there must be a great deal. Schools, it seems, cannot just be called schools, they have to have a handle attached. I mentioned in the second chapter that Gallows Road Primary could now very well be called Gallows Road Primary School, Nursery and Space Technology College. I was not joking, this is actually happening.

Some schools build up justifiable reputations in certain subject areas. It may be music, technology or dance, perhaps. Some heads will waste no time in having this emblazed on the front of the school. What they are forgetting, however, is that often this reputation has been built up by with the blood, sweat and tears of one enthusiastic and dedicated person. When that person leaves, what happens? The simple fact is that the standard in that area is, to put it politely, not maintained. The title however remains for evermore.

Heads are extremely faddish creatures. If they see a school with some wonderful innovation they have to have it in their school, *now*! Gallows Road has a stunning school band. We must have one too. Gallows Road has a wonderful nature area, so will we. Listening to Mozart in their maths lessons has really improved their results. We'll listen to Bach as well. The list goes on. The problem is, however, the consequences of these fads lie about the school for a long time. Boxes of broken recorders in music rooms, heaps of unboxed and scratched CDs on staffroom shelves, abandoned nature areas and piles of cracked flower pots, all that remains of the gardening club. All in their time were good ideas, but unless there is the person/people to maintain them they will fade away.

The media are partly to blame for the advance of strange ideas. You will probably have noticed that certain schools have a regular presence in the local free paper. You will probably have wondered how the school manages to find the staff to maintain all these clubs and societies. The very simple answer is that usually they don't; they are as ephemeral as a mayfly in spring. Surely if something is good enough to begin it is good enough to continue. It should not just be on a sudden flight of fancy of the person supposedly in control.

Onward and upward

> So you want to get on in the trade,
> Reap rewards for the effort you've made,
> If you have a notion
> To secure your promotion
> Make sure your foundation's well laid.

As you totally ignored my words of warning in the Prologue, I presume there is absolutely no point in trying to put you off thoughts of promotion. However, if you are enjoying the job you may as well make a move to where you can do a bit of good outside the four walls of your classroom. If you decide to embark on this course it is important that you start planning your moves early in your career. A little bit like an extended game of chess, really. Once again, follow the basic rules and you could go far.

I'll try and make the pathway as simple as possible, but before we go on just one word of warning. If you can't stand paperwork, staff meetings, (or for that matter meetings of any sort), listening to people lecturing who do not know a fraction of what they think they do, or sitting on committees, forget it.

At one time the promotion to headship was the pinnacle of any teacher's ambition. Headship was achieved by rising through the ranks from classroom teacher to coordinator, head of department perhaps, and then reaching the penultimate step of deputy. Heads were not overly immersed in administration, as is the case now, but had the time to take an active part in the real business of school life, namely, teaching. My first head taught French to every class in the school, this being one of the latest educational fads of the 1970s. In my second school the boss taught for fifty per cent of the timetable and, I hasten to add, enjoyed every minute of it. Many head teachers found the time to attend every single football/cricket/rounders match. Even more important, however, they were able to instil into the school a little of their own character.

This was all brought to an end by the introduction of LMS, Local Management of Schools.

LMS was supposed to give to heads the opportunity to manage their own budgets so that schools were not tied to the whims of the LEAs. At first glance, what a good idea; but as is always the case with poorly thought through changes several things started to go wrong. First, many of the old school of head teachers had no experience of managing the considerable budgets of schools. They were in fact terrified of the whole idea. I lost count of the number of times I heard head teachers say, 'I am a teacher, albeit a head one, not a bloody accountant!' This resulted in many of them taking refuge in early retirement, or not infrequently, changes in career. Many heads, I am sorry to say, suffered real health problems caused by the stress of the excessive work load put on them.

However, you are not going to be a head teacher straight away, even though their average age seems to be decreasing yearly, and you will need to follow the approved series of promotion steps that happen to be place at the time. These seem to change by the week, so there is no point in being too specific.

There is one overriding factor that you have to bear in mind at all times, and that is the matter of good old evidence. Whatever you do in school, whether it be breaking wind during a staff meeting or turning up to a Home and School Association meeting, make a record of it. If you go on a course or lead a group in staff training sessions, put it in your diary, (I would recommend a special gilt-edged leather volume for this), and whenever you can get an official-looking piece of paper, get it signed by somebody who thinks they are important; at a pinch the head teacher will do.

Attend as many courses as you possibly can and make sure, at every available opportunity, that you point out how useful the course was. Volunteer to lead a staff meeting and 'cascade' (a popular term in the 1990s) all you learned to your audience, that is if they happen to be awake. Always be willing to take the morning assembly. This will definitely put you in the head's good books, hence improving your reference, and if you can make them good long ones you will certainly be flavour of the month with the rest of the staff. Doing a stint as staff representative on the school's Board of Governors will help to get your name and face known, and will also let you see some of the machinations of school government.

Start applying for jobs as soon as is decently possible. I would recommend trying after the first couple of years. There are no points given whatsoever for staying in one school for any great length of time. Despite saying this, I spent fourteen years in my first school and sixteen years in my second. Needless to say, although I was very happy, I did not progress very far up the career ladder. If you actually get shortlisted for an interview, consider this a success whether you get the job or not. Interview technique is important, more important in fact than how good you are as a teacher.

One final plea. If you reach the dizzy heights, please remember what I have said. Yes, children are the raisons d'être of our profession or trade. But a happy, well-appreciated staff will result in happy children and a happy, well-balanced, school. One little bit of advice I was given by my first head was that the very best thing to do first in a new job is absolutely nothing. I sincerely wish that every PDH would follow this little maxim…

Anyway, the very best of luck, and proceed to my final farewell.

The Epilogue

> Don't let what I've tried to relate
> Put you off; it can truly be great.
> Despite interference
> You can make a difference
> So go for it, children can't wait.

I wrote the Prologue to this little work some time ago in a fit of pique. It was originally intended to be a 'venting of the spleen' on matters educational, but just like Topsy it has 'growed and growed'. However there are, I feel, a few points that I think should be clarified.

First, and most important, I still love teaching. There is nothing quite like the buzz you get when you see the light of understanding dawn in a child's eye or the pride they show when performing a musical piece in front of their parents. I think that it is this feeling that has kept a good many teachers in the classroom and not hunting for another career. My closing comment in the Prologue was that I was getting out of education. The fact of the matter is that I can't really imagine a life without some involvement in teaching.

Secondly, everything you read here is actually based on what I have experienced both as a full-time and supply teacher, although when putting it on to paper I have kept my tongue firmly in my cheek. If any of you reading this are teachers you will probably recognise many of the examples and probably be able to top them all with your own experiences.

I have had draft copies of this little document perused by friends and colleagues who I can trust, and without fail the response has been, 'How true!' – often with a request for signed copies in the event of its publication. I would recommend that as you start your career keep, a careful note of all the 'interesting' little events you encounter, and perhaps in thirty-eight years' time you will produce your own volume. I doubt that I shall be round to enjoy it, but you never know.

Finally if you recognise yourself on these pages, don't blame me! All the people, places situations and events described are real, only the names have been changed.

If you are not a teacher but are considering taking up the chalk/white board marker/smart board pen, I hope I have not put you off completely. Take what was said in the opening pages with a large pinch of salt. I would strongly suggest that you spend some time working with children in a voluntary capacity. Teaching is a craft, which I believe suits some more than others. I have known people with no qualifications whatsoever hold a class enthralled and I have also seen fully trained teachers with some years' experience deliver the most deadly boring lesson imaginable.

I am now working in a bit of a cloud cuckoo land situation as ninety-five per cent of my work is as a supply teacher. I can wave a cheery farewell to teachers on staff meeting days and happily ignore the coarse responses I often get. On the whole, planning, assessment and the writing of reports are the thing of the past, and I can sleep the sleep of the blameless the nights before parents' evenings. I now have time to indulge more in my hobbies, and of course have managed to produce this little opus.

Perhaps in years to come a little sanity will return to schools, and the government will manage to keep their hands off matters educational. For the moment, however, try to enjoy the job, do your best to keep your head above the murky waters of paperwork and, for the time being, farewell.

Postscript

Our leaders, whom we should admire,
Have little that one could desire:
Their plans pedagogic
Reveal little logic
And their actions just fill one with ire.

Appendix: List of Education Ministers

The following list shows all the Ministers of Education since 1945. I have put an asterix by two of them. Can anyone tell me why? Answer at the bottom of the list.

- Rab Butler (3 August 1944–25 May 1945)
- Richard Law (25 May 1945–26 July 1945)
- Ellen Wilkinson (3 August 1945–6 February 1947) (died in office)
- George Tomlinson (10 February 1947–26 October 1951)
- Florence Horsbrugh (2 November 1951–18 October 1954)
- David Eccles (18 October 1954–13 January 1957)
- Viscount Hailsham (13 January 1957–17 September 1957)
- Geoffrey Lloyd (17 September 1957–14 October 1959)
- David Eccles (14 October 1959–13 July 1962)
- Sir Edward Boyle (13 July 1962–1 April 1964)
- Quintin Hogg (formerly Viscount Hailsham) (1 April 1964–16 October 1964)
- Michael Stewart (18 October 1964–22 January 1965)
- Anthony Crosland (22 January 1965–29 August 1967)
- Patrick Gordon Walker (29 August 1967–6 April 1968)
- Edward Short (6 April 1968–19 June 1970)
- Margaret Thatcher (20 June 1970–4 March 1974)
- Reginald Prentice (5 March 1974–10 June 1975)
- Fred Mulley (10 June 1975–10 September 1976)

- Shirley Williams (10 September 1976–4 May 1979)
- Mark Carlisle (5 May 1979–14 September 1981)
- Sir Keith Joseph, Bt. (14 September 1981–21 May 1986)
- Kenneth Baker (21 May 1986–24 July 1989)
- John MacGregor (24 July 1989–2 November 1990)
- Kenneth Clarke (2 November 1990–10 April 1992)
- John Patten (10 April 1992–20 July 1994)
- Gillian Shepherd (5 July 1995–2 May 1997) ★
- David Blunkett (2 May 1997–8 June 2001)
- Estelle Morris (8 June 2001–24 October 2002) (resigned)★
- Charles Clarke (24 October 2002–15 December 2004)
- Ruth Kelly (15 December 2004–5 May 2006)
- Alan Johnson (5 May 2006–27 June 2007)
- Ed Balls (since 28 June 2007)

Answer:

Gillian Shepherd and Estelle Morris, who resigned, are the only Secretaries of State for Education with any significant experience of teaching. We wonder why things go wrong!

Printed in Great Britain
by Amazon.co.uk, Ltd.,
Marston Gate.